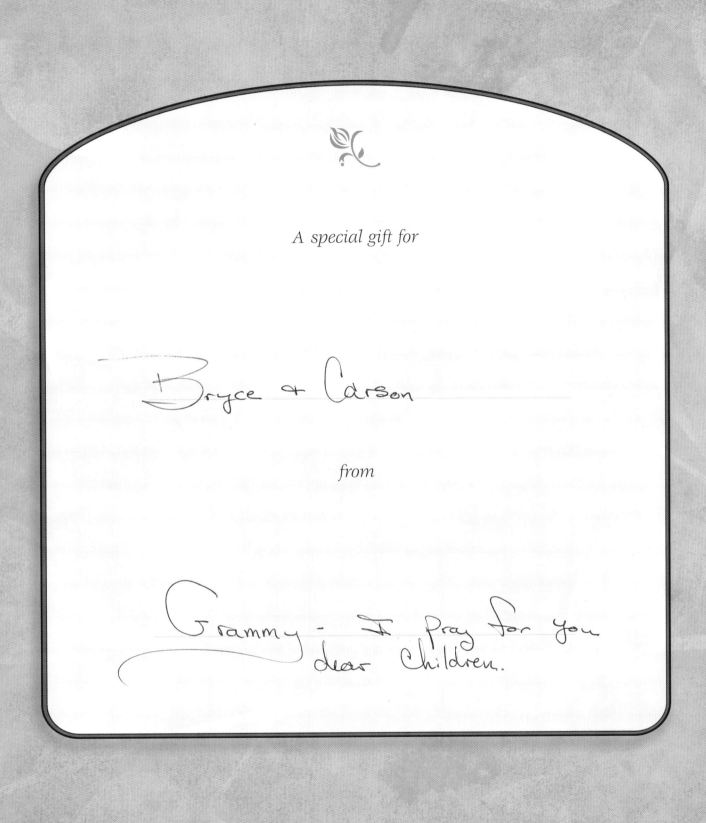

A special gift for

*Bryce & Carson*

from

*Grammy - I Pray for you
dear children.*

# Grandma, What is Prayer?

Katherine Bohlmann ❧ Illustrations by Jan Naimo Jones

CPH
SAINT LOUIS

Scripture quotations taken from the HOLY BIBLE, NEW INTERNATIONAL VERSION®. NIV®.
Copyright © 1973, 1978, 1984 by International Bible Society.
Used by permission of Zondervan Publishing House. All rights reserved.

Text copyright © 2002 Katherine Bohlmann
Illustrations copyright © 2002 Jan Naimo Jones

Published by Concordia Publishing House
3558 S. Jefferson Avenue, St. Louis, MO 63118-3968
Manufactured in China

All rights reserved. No part of this publication may be reproduced,
stored in a retrieval system, or transmitted, in any form or by any means,
electronic, mechanical, photocopying, recording, or otherwise,
without the prior written permission of Concordia Publishing House.

1  2  3  4  5  6  7  8  9  10        11  10  09  08  07  06  05  04  03  02

**This book is dedicated to all the grandmothers of my family who helped us learn how to pray.**

Marjorie Bohlmann

Jean MacKain

Wanda Heitmeyer

Marie Kimmel

Irene Matthews

Gertrude Bohlmann

"Grandma, what are you doing there?
I see your hands are folded in prayer.
The table isn't even set,
And it's not time for bed just yet."

"Yes, my child, it's good to pray,
At mealtimes or at end of day.
But other times our prayers ascend;
We're not to let our prayer time end."

"Grandma, tell me, how can this be?"

"Let's look in the Bible, then we'll see."

*Pray continually.* 1 Thessalonians 5:17

"Grandma, I can't always pray—
I'm not in church every single day.
Is there somewhere I can be
Where I know God is hearing me?"

"Church is not the only place
To pray to God or seek His grace.
God shows His children His great care.
He wants us to pray everywhere."

"Grandma, tell me, how can this be?"

"Let's look in the Bible, then we'll see."

*And pray ...*
*on all occasions with all kinds of prayers*
*and requests.  Ephesians 6:18*

"But if I can go anywhere,
I still don't see the need for prayer.
Not just at bedtime anymore …
So, Grandma, tell me, what's prayer for?"

"God wants to hear all of our cares;
Our wants and needs go in our prayers.
Also our thanks and praise we send,
In Jesus' name to God, our Friend."

"Grandma, tell me, how can this be?"

"Let's look in the Bible, then we'll see."

*Cast all your anxiety on Him*
*because He cares for you.* 1 Peter 5:7

"Grandma, tell me why we pray
To God our Father every day.
If we've no worries or no cares,
What should we ask for in our prayers?"

"We can pray for others, too.
There's still more God wants us to do:
Pray for help when tempted to sin,
And for help with trouble we're in."

"Grandma, tell me, how can this be?"

"Let's look in the Bible, then we'll see."

*Therefore confess your sins to each other and pray for each other so that you may be healed.* James 5:16

*"Watch and pray so that you will not fall into temptation. The spirit is willing, but the body is weak."* Matthew 26:41

*Is any one of you in trouble? He should pray.* James 5:13a

"Grandma, tell me how to pray—
I don't know what words to say.
What if I say something wrong?
What if my prayer's too short or long?"

"It doesn't matter when you end.
Talk to God just like a friend.
He understands just what you say.
Jesus taught us a prayer to pray."

"Grandma, tell me, how can this be?"

"Let's look in the Bible, then we'll see."

*[Jesus said,] "This, then, is how you should pray: 'Our Father in heaven, hallowed be Your name, Your kingdom come, Your will be done on earth as it is in heaven. Give us today our daily bread. Forgive us our debts, as we also have forgiven our debtors. And lead us not into temptation, but deliver us from the evil one.' "*

Matthew 6:9–13

"But Grandma, what if God won't hear,
When to Him I bring prayers near?
Maybe God's too busy for me—
What a sad thing that would be."

"God has promised that He'll hear
His own children far and near.
He's not too busy, our God above;
Our answered prayers show us His love."

"Grandma, tell me, how can this be?"

"Let's look in the Bible, then we'll see."

*"Call to Me and I will answer you ..."* Jeremiah 33:3

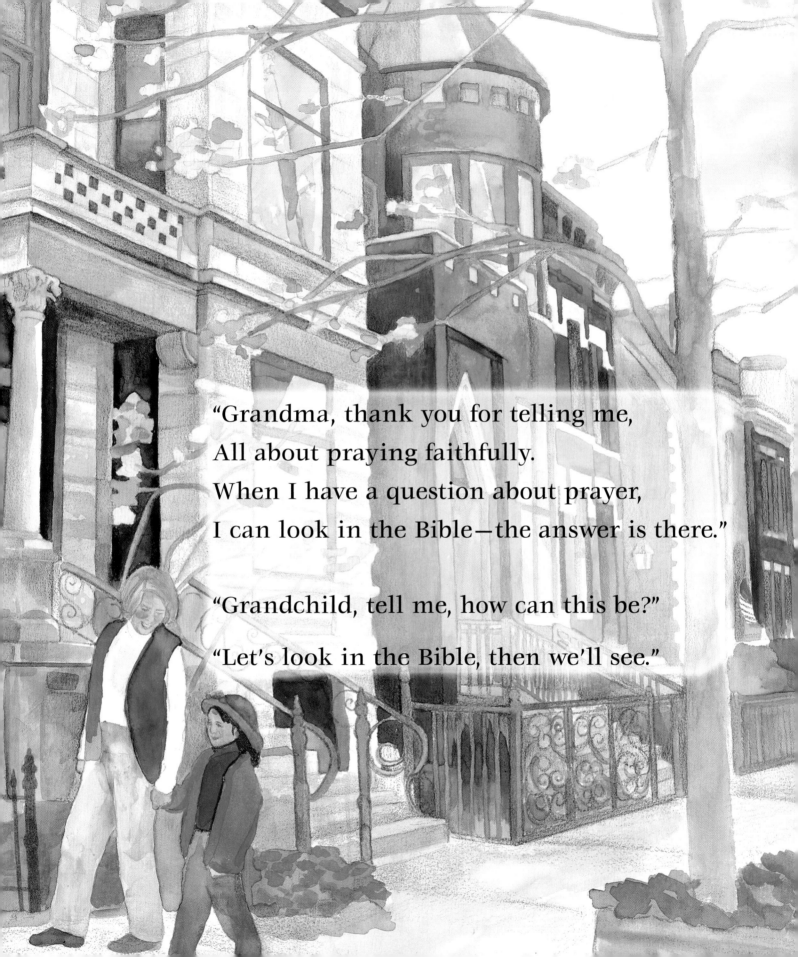

"Grandma, thank you for telling me,
All about praying faithfully.
When I have a question about prayer,
I can look in the Bible—the answer is there."

"Grandchild, tell me, how can this be?"

"Let's look in the Bible, then we'll see."

*All Scripture is God-breathed and
is useful for teaching, rebuking, correcting,
and training in righteousness.*

2 Timothy 3:16